The Gaza of Winter

THE GAZA OF
WINTER

Poems by
Donald Revell

The University of Georgia Press

Athens and London

© 1988 by Donald Revell
Published by the University of Georgia Press
Athens, Georgia 30602
All rights reserved
Designed by Betty McDaniel
Set in Linotron Meridien
The paper in this book meets the guidelines for
permanence and durability of the Committee on
Production Guidelines for Book Longevity of the
Council on Library Resources.

Printed in the United States of America

92 91 90 89 88   5 4 3 2 1

Library of Congress Cataloging in Publication Data

Revell, Donald, 1954–
The Gaza of winter: poems/by Donald Revell.
p.   cm.
ISBN 0-8203-0988-5 (alk. paper).
ISBN 0-8203-0989-3 (pbk.: alk. paper)
I. Title.
PS3568.E793G3   1988
811'.54—dc19
87-12523
CIP

British Library Cataloging in Publication Data available.

To Dennis Finnell

The publication of this book is supported by a grant
from the National Endowment for the Arts,
a federal agency.

Acknowledgments

The author and the publisher gratefully acknowledge the following publications in which poems for this volume first appeared, often in substantially different form.

American Poetry Review: "Consenting," "Eumenides," "Fauviste," "Futurist," "At the Exhibition of Parables," "The Siege of the City of Gorky"

Antaeus: "Maestro"

Antioch Review: "A Setting"

Chariton Review: "Descriptive Quality," "The Backyard in August"

Crazyhorse: "Extracts: For Céline"

Denver Quarterly: "The Melville Scholar," "The More Lustrous," "Birthplace"

Indiana Review: "A Home Made Saint"

New England Review/Bread Loaf Quarterly: "Charleston," "Gaza" (as "Divorce Pending"), "Beloved Author and the New State"

Paris Review: "The Gaza of Winter," "Why History Imitates God"

Pequod: "The Next Marriage," "A Heart's Instruments," "Prague"

Poet and Critic: "The Children's Undercroft"

Poetry: "Car Radio," "To Penelope"

Poetry East: "Emily Dickinson's Mirror, Amherst"

Sonora Review: "The Ways There Are"

Tar River Poetry: "Cézanne"

"A Setting" also appeared in the prize anthology *The Pushcart Prize X.*

Contents

I. Coursework

II. Accounting

III.   Clearing Away

I
Coursework

The Ways There Are

As you drive up to the sign that reads "El Dorado,"
looking past it to the row of orange
gnomes and houses it stands for, you feel caught.
It's Christmas, and the gnomes hold big wreaths.
One has a lightbulb wired to his orange face,
and in the staggering flashes he seems
to tell you something about how to end the year
on a country road near El Dorado.
"Hold your wreath. Stand still and slip out of history."

There is more behind you now than ever,
now that a long year of crazy developments
has put you out upon the roads at Christmas.
More of the signs seem heartsick and familiar.
From the car, those gnomes look like a memorial
to everyone. This past October, your big hero
disappeared into one of his own letters
about towns and the disasters towns use
for charm. The flashing gnome is for him.

The others hold their wreaths in the dark and honor
all that's scattered in the months behind you:
the floating girls, the specimen days and trials.
You have made hardly anything of them.
In the scared rush that carries you, one girl
turns into another and both leave.
The days do likewise. As for the trials,

you win them all and so cannot excuse
your ending up in tears on a country road.

You drive off, keeping the flashing gnome in your mirror.
Naming him to yourself, you think of all
the ways there are to get out of going on
to the next town, the next real city of gold
that floats along on the back of any sad
event or holiday. Your hero's dead.
It's Christmas, and history, the days you've spent
in advance and still need, carries you, knowing
the name of the next place it will put you down.

IN MEMORY OF RICHARD HUGO

Birthplace

Looking for one hand waving out of the shadowbox
of streets, the staggered cars and railings,
lights hesitating between the shifts of wind,

I do not find it. Designed for no one,
no effect in mind, these fronts and disappearing
corners are as dour as they are plainly habitable.

They confine the street fiercely.
They limit it to those unresponding,
defaced versions of itself I cannot change.

A place to be used, impossible to really love
except as a thing survived, a scar.
And what I do not find here confirms more

than the blankness of one street. These metal awnings,
these Virgins tilting beside the failed trees and ashcans,
pronounce the end of an idea: that people,

given the raw materials and time,
will shape a place to their needs, will lift it up
along the bright curve of their shared, best hopes.

The people here hoped only to stay on.
Taught only to arrive, to get this far
and no farther, they could not imagine

any use in altering a haven that worked
so well it buried them. Between the shifts of wind,
they are proved right, and I do not exist.

The Children's Undercroft

In rooms beneath the church, we stood up singing.
We marched behind our little cross in time
to the yellow keys of someone's cast-off spinet,
wishing we were upstairs under the big cross.
The light was ordinary as it fell in
through plain windows near the ceiling.
We kept thinking of the adults and of *their* windows—
angels and doves in blood-red clouds. We marched
and waited to march up to the real kingdom.

If there are many mansions, there are many
rooms, surely. The ones I'm thinking of now
were a brown cluster of alcoves named for whatever
child saint, crowned and smiling under its cracked
bell jar, each contained. We were assigned
to alcoves by grades. After the hymns and marching,
we would gather around our saints in folding chairs
and learn to be just like them, to merit, like them,
an eternity of crowned, famous smiling.

It was a lesson that would not end, even
when we had folded up our chairs and stacked them
in the last ritual of our small Sunday.
Perfection, fame, and an ecstatic death
seemed all of a piece. Anything less, anything
as stained and usual as our own lives,
was an impoverishment we could not imagine

and had to live with anyway. It would drag
through unremarkable events toward nothing

happy. For us, as we stood waiting
among the crooked stones of the churchyard to be taken
home, eternity would either come soon
or in time only to be more of the same
anxious, unecstatic marching.
Every Sunday, the spinet would sound more
cast-off. Our easy hymns would become dull
or silly. Overrehearsed, we would at last
enter the real kingdom unmoved and not sing.

The Siege of the City of Gorky

I have no trouble staying inside the lines
and small corners of things, wanting only to be with you
as the storm abates, as the household animals
stop whining and go out into the streets.
There are so many good mouths in corners, such sirens.
And I have no trouble speaking as they speak
now that the sky is clear and the dark mist
of police and animal noise has rolled on.
I am not with you. I hate no government.
I hate only those with no eyes for the weather.

Over the back wall of the garden
all the cool shapes of the storm tumble
into other worlds where you are still not waiting.
Imagine their disappointment, the hard outline
of their lives there. I have no trouble saying,
in the lawless, half-baked language of those lives,
that I have studied hard, more than the police,
more than the animals, to be prepared
for what comes—storm, drought, or the famine of mouths
opened to heat lightning and no word from you.

Late autumn. Hearing a noise, I look outside.
Over the back wall of the garden
a storm the size of a small woman gathers
leaves in a pretty funnel. I watch
until the hard ground is cleared and the funnel
choked with leaves. I want a wife badly,

knowing that there will be no word from you,
that the police, animals, and storms of the beautiful
city of Gorky are the only mouths on my mouth,
my mother tongue the whirling noise of leaves.

Eumenides

So many accidents of detail are a vengeance.
The accurate still life of an hour, or rooms
shunted along a hallway in the Bronx
press hard, and you can feel the air giving way.

The freakish cloak and dagger of light gives way
also. And I am left to chart a course
through so much collapse and all the angry dealings
of nights urging their dark corners of the news

on me that I mistake everything, believe
everything, and run blind. Whatever love was,
it has changed to a crazy line through darkness.
Each turn shows one other face that turns

up smiling hard, like Niobe or my Anne,
pointing a way past vengeance I can't see.
I redouble back through hours and rooms, thinking
whether any story of mine would leave me here.

I can remember only so much
at once, acknowledge only one
wrong course at a time before the whole
thing gets scary, and a scattering
of features of real events becomes
one hurt face. There was the hour I
sat quiet, letting Anne grieve for want
of no word I could offer. The light

stalled between us. Her hands, two shadows
folded on the table near a bowl
of shadows, looked already passed over
into some chiaroscuro
of my silence and her grief.
The acutest sense of any hour
is that hour, accurate enough
over the long haul to make nonsense
of ten years. Or of the one hurt face
of my home, rooms yellowing beside
each other above the yellow blotch
of the street and its sharp noise. That place
resurfaces in the oblique,
loose matters of detail in any
place I feel wrong. Those rooms strip all others
bare. They turn the Bronx into
someone else's dream I can neither
end nor change nor keep from recounting
at all the worst times. And now I'm scared.
Only so much of that part
of everything that is really vengeance
has a name. The rest is waiting
in the wings, an accident
just now getting ready to happen.

Anything can turn furious. The crazy
line through wreckage that wears my face and all
the faces seems not to end. And on the way,
even the most damaged things have one

surface glazed, a sudden distorting mirror
that I can't help finding. There, I look as I did

stalled in hours or places it is shame
to remember. The Eumenides are slow

vengeance, meted out anywhere love fails
in the collapse and angry dealings of self-love.
The light presses. The air presses hard and no
story of mine is good enough to hold out.

What I could not help, I have denied.
The yellow rooms in the Bronx. My Anne
expecting grief to find words I did not have.
And there is more, just now getting ready to happen.

Gaza

Its weight is a flawless shadow of lilacs—
accurate, straight-edged as my name by yours,
and as routine as imagining our children.

Every night, I pull that shadow uphill
in a long dray against a current of children
who do not know me and have rooms of their own

in tenements all over the loud hill.
They go there to make love and feel important.
Afterwards, they go to the windows. There

I am, two or three flights down in the street,
a vendor of shadow flowers sharp as razors.
They go back to bed. I could have been their father.

A Home Made Saint

The New Year's sound of birds is my beginning
to learn that youth is disloyalty in ways
this first morning of the year cannot survive.
I am widowed there. I need to begin
myself over for the sake of the birds.

I will change anything, no matter how good.
The name of my best friend. The shape of the hills
in the window of this spare room in my best friend's house.
I have been happy here, and that is no good.
Swear to nothing. Let birds make all the noise.

One year ago in this same room,
Anne and I woke to a new year in that window,
those same hills sparkling under the sound of birds.
No use knowing now where she has gone.
No song or window should ever be that clear.

If I could count on one thing in the white months
crowded in front of me, it would be speechless.
Something like lilacs. I would say to it
that summer is an ocean, autumn a shoreline
harrowed by loud birds that destroy lilacs.

I would say it quickly and stick to my story.
Oh Anne, my calendar, my embrace
of sparrows mocking me with quick wings,

this morning I was thinking about birds
and they sang. And then they flew off.

Nothing could have been simpler or more faithless.
I will always be older than the birds and always
wait at the year's end for their accidental
demand that I begin myself over.
I will never age or be abandoned again.

At the Exhibition of Parables

I have the address exactly. I know her name.
Right now, the espaliered wood-rose, a lampwork
of flowers and trained birds, is falling
out of her yard and into traffic. I am too late
to see it torn apart by three cars.
The flattened petals and displaced birds;
Balkanized, unlucky address by Anne's name.

The new polity is a collective of small
hearts biding out of reach among hybrid flowers.
It has relocated the past to suburbs
I cannot bear. Anne used to wake early,
would go down quietly into the yard to shape
the trees into candelabra. On the worst night,
she set them ablaze. The fires spread to the house.

The new polity enjoyed the change. Anne
moved far away into a smaller house
in a warm climate that did not use fires.
I remember she had freckled hands year round
and in the hot months the fingers darkened
like rose twigs so heavy with roses
they snap into pieces in a hard rain.

Everything must be set ablaze to be seen.
And then a hard rain comes and the maps
are redrawn to explain the ashes, the old borders
buried under heaps of roses.

They are poor Anne's fingers. The new maps
show not even a single country with her name,
no border of flowers that resembles her.

Anne is elsewhere. I have the exact
address and know how she lives. At first light,
she tends to the wood-rose, teaching it to grow
into a lamp that burns flowers and beautiful
trained birds one night in its lifetime. Right now
she is safe indoors. There is a new polity.
It is a murderous traffic of small hearts.

The More Lustrous

So many things arrive as themselves and need
no witnesses. Complete under the fretted,
bronze glare of city nights or in the sudden,
flat light of the country, they are already
beyond us. They are unvarying, and as
they appear, we break ourselves to pieces against them.

One time, Central Park was covered in new snow
and I walked all the way across it, meeting
nobody. It was my best day, the one
I always use in my letters home and look for,
year after year, when I go back or see
New York in a movie. It will never turn up.

It will persist as a detail remembered
out of context, daring me to fit
it into some good story I can't imagine.
Always, the same adamantine buildings
rise up out of the bare trees as I
make nothing out of them except a romance

in which I do not appear. And so even the best
day is a light to fail by, and my joy
a lucent hazard I cannot avoid
too long. Too often, it is as if that hazard
moved, staying one step ahead of me. This morning,
I walked back into the field behind my house

and one patch of sky was a blue screen receding
across the bare ground, leaving a wild design
of settled birds and thin ice in the furrows.
There was no place for me anywhere in that field.
But as I stood there, an unnecessary,
glad witness, I kept trying to think of one.

Cézanne

What else is there to know but the primed surface
of the air latticed between things? Bands of light,
the changing shadows fretted like green chevrons
onto the lilacs, the guttering, half-white

rain—all emerge from that and return as one
elaborate, dark wash, the complete day.
At a window over the bright yard, what darkens
is a thought reshaped to air and the arriving

storm. I will take it down among the lilacs,
hoping to watch it disappear as they do,
into the wide latticework and near
sense of things preparing to emerge.

II
Accounting

A Setting

There is nothing Orphic, nothing foreign.
The deep greens of a suburban June,
the lawns, the orientalia,
are enough, for now, to make you sing.

The deep greens of a suburban June
drift from oriel to oriel and
are enough, for now, to make you sing
into the dark you've watched

drift from oriel to oriel. And
now the air around the porchlights curves
into the dark you've watched,
changing into the colored air of romance.

Now the air around the porchlights curves
like hours in summer, like desire,
changing into the colored air of romance
your first home breathed into you.

Like hours in summer, like desire,
what you cried out each June
your first home breathed into you,
became the best of you.

What you cried out each June—
"There is nothing Orphic, nothing foreign!"—
became the best of you,
the lawns, the orientalia.

IN MEMORY OF JOHN CHEEVER

The Melville Scholar

The flowers I sent outlived you by three days.
They were white roses and had a card that read
"Please, sir, a chapter about all this whiteness."
You would have obliged, but had already taken
yourself over into a silence
you would not break, a whiteness more complete
than that of roses or hospitals
or of the thousand miles of snow between us that day
you died. You would have written to me that nothing
is as true as a blank page, or as accurate.
You would also have been careful to append
a list of ways one might avoid saying so,
a program for a happy career in fiction.

Death is a blank fact to be told the same way,
over and over. But its untelling,
the fiction, lives as we do not, from change to change,
grander with every step away from those facts
it has refused. It is a sweeping gesture
of disbelief we cannot afford, but need.
I may be years untelling what you began
with a question. What is any book or any life
but a monster with a dozen names?
And in pursuing that monster, in demanding
that every one of its names be given a story,
you discovered that no one name is right,
that no one story is the true account

of them all. You made your own life over then
into a quest you had to scorn or die to complete.
Compelled either to believe in no word's
honest version of the truth or in every word,
you looked towards silence, hoping that it
would be the great white name of all names
and your vindication. What I will need to untell
is that you even wanted vindicating.
I will have to restore the careless freedom of false
speech to every gesture and idea
you professed, if only to belie your last gesture,
the chapter that you did not send,
the loving fiction you could not disbelieve.

Fauviste

Five minutes with his paintings and I remember.
This is life on the boats, and any place
to stand is a dead wife bobbing under daubs
of wet lanterns, not a thought of home,
no imagining how the three beds
of iris will burst and stand beside the house.

Five minutes, and I cannot picture my own life.

I don't think there is any use looking backward.
The boats were lowered by other hands than mine
as I slept. When I awoke, we were already
far from the sinking and had new names.
My wife was dead or in love with someone else
in another boat. At night, we strung up lanterns
and we had five minutes of a beautiful painting.

We were never rescued. And I am sure
that rescue only happens to the faithful,
that seeing five minutes of the world with no wife
and all the lanterns hanging close to the water
changed my eyes into other things that see
but cannot see rescue when it comes.

I see my wife and flowers in everyone's hands.

I don't think there is any use painting irises.
The three beds that I know my wife tended

were lost at sea. Their petals washed towards land
and into the mouths of rivers painted by Frenchmen.
I cannot picture them. I only know that they fell to pieces
as I slept and that someone in France made something
out of them that is my life on the boats.

Extracts: For Céline

"In one dream, I have only to throw a twig
to kill you. Fallen, you arise as a winged
shade keening through Europe, through a lengthening
succession of rooms and fields I want to save,
that you burn." To some things, neither a lament

nor any compensation matters. Years
succeed each other as a column of bound men.
To some things, the unloving preserve
of common nightmare is safe haven,
is past loss. I think of rooms and fields dressed out

in that complete responsiveness I need
to expect from places. They are all afire now.
They diminish, drawing themselves down
into a dark core I cannot enter. They
are beyond responding, an old world, the next.

And so hating all of it is not completely
senseless perhaps, if only as a way
of carrying off one livid feeling
into exile. Hating the faithlessness
of anything that goes on, you can hope

for what has to happen anyway: the torches,
the cries in the streets and on the country roads.
"In this dream, the sky is falling into pieces.

In the confusion, I can hear a voice
as flat as a travelogue's. It narrates, moving

calmly from scene to scene as though the end
of everything were a routine kindness, part
of a more intricate or grander gesture."
There are some things I cannot hope for.
There are other responses, other compensations.

The Gaza of Winter

The frail smoke and virtues of the season blind
us, almost with hands, and which of us can instruct
the other now? I will have to find your body
shifting at the edge of your last word.
You will have to find whatever I could mean
by groping along that same edge. And all of winter
will be ground to nothing in a slow mill

of smoke and virtue. We are bound to that mill
and our cold seeking and shifting is the blind
set task of that bondage, cruellest in winter.
What does it matter that we love and instruct
our hearts rightly? I have lost the way to your body.
You have lost the way to know what I mean
when I curl up inside every word

you speak as if it were your hand. A word
is as close as I can ever come. This winter,
we have been forced to understand the blind
distance between virtue and a body
bound up in nothing it could ever mean.
A marriage is Gaza. Ours is blind at a mill
now, every turn of which seems meant to instruct

the dark in darkening, hearts in how to instruct
themselves in spite. There will be blanks instead of words
from now on, a grist of silence for the mill.
But why is it I still think of going blind

with you as my life's work? In our first winter,
I followed you up the steps to where your body
slipped out of grey ice and lit the mean

rooms wonderfully. What would happen if those mean
rooms turned up again, a few steps from the mill
we turn? Would anything about them instruct
us in how to live there as we did, all winter,
curled up in the smoke and virtue of blind
first nights and first days? I wish that every word
I knew were a step back to them. A body

should give off more than light if anybody
is to go on thinking of it not meaning
to go crazy. I should do more with the words
I know than make puzzles. A life's work can instruct
a life or can lead it in bondage to a mill
of bad marriage, bad silence, and a blind
refusal to accept that in one winter

everything can go right, then wrong. The winter
I followed you up your steps is over. Your body
is wrapped up in its own words now and cannot mean
what I wish it did. I think of years of mill
work ahead, grinding down a store of words
you will not hear me say, living to instruct
a puzzled heart in how to live blind.

Why History Imitates God

The near past and the near future are poor
with no accession of hands, no bright legs—
useless, untender absences with bronze torsoes.
Each day, there is the hollow of good works
and inside that, an hour with the statues
I have collected of such hard torsoes,
parts of bodies I cannot comfort
with hands and legs, features and good works.
For my own comfort, I press my face against them.
It makes the bronze strange and that eases
the occult poverty of the hour,
a body smaller than mine. I'm poor. My house
has no hands or legs and the near silence
of the statues dies away as I move closer.

I like to believe that they were never children,
just as the near past and future never
lift their hands to the ribbons of a swing
or look to their mother, a distorted face
captured in the hard mirrors of bronzes.
I like to believe I say the things I must
the only way possible. I have a house.
It is poor. The way I feel about time is poor.
One hour in any direction looks starved
or distorted with anger, like the face
of the good woman I refuse to remember
although a part of her body is repeated

many times in the next room, her limbs
the tenderness and silence of other houses.

It is time to know what everyone not wasted
in childhood knows. The body is too many
pieces, scattered among inexpressive
desires too strong and spiteful to end
anywhere but the poorhouse, the shanty museum
of torsoes. I am no child and wasted nothing
in childhood that might explain this poverty
of cold change from hour to hour, from body
to one more casting of the same body
I will never use. I do not want my life.
It is safer elsewhere with limbs, in other houses.
I want to be set free in the next room
to press my face against the strange heat
of bronze whose silence could not love me less.

No Valediction

I want to uncurve us from the bedpost's polished
glass and cannot. We stay there, flailing just
beneath the surface of the light we darken
with dark eyes and our bodies using the light
to flail. The bedroom window is all sky.
If I could fill it with you, I'd be alone.

In the mornings, I remember less than ever.
The days lie straight out of the room and only
begin to curve hours later, turning away
from every surface polished enough to catch light
or the two of us as we still are.
If this goes on for long, I will always love you.

To Penelope

Nothing impossible as this one solitude
and what's to be made of it. I thought a word
like "freedom" or phrases like "the end of the heart"
would give it wheels and a driver to drive home
and me balled-up in the dark, where it keeps raining.

Solitude is no rain in Florida and no inn.
Night falls. The sky sets fire to the ground
and all night in the back seat of the drought
everything is so defamed the stars die.
No getting home. No grasping the right end

of freedom and tossing it out of the car.
I might keep listening for the rain forever,
balled-up in the dark with no driver, seeing
nowhere I have ever lived with you
looming ahead and the front door opening.

In Florida, I keep house with strangers.
I show your photograph to everyone.
Your eyes worry, and the house, streaked black with rain
behind you, is so much empty space and so lost
that I have nothing to say to keep you

posed there, looking into the camera
for the right end of your heart or for your freedom.
The picture can be of two minds, can go crazy.

Its half-toned, parting obscenity
curls at the edges and is nothing like

ourselves waiting to be together, out of the rain.
Nothing impossible as this one solitude.
I have the photograph to prove it
and to prove I can't help wishing we were there
after the long drought, eyes streaked black with rain.

Consenting

In your best dream, everything responds
and smiles with the loving awkwardness,
the sudden, blurred readjustments of
a group photograph. There is a word
for everyone. There is a sky
filled with the tops of trees and letters
hanging from them, spelling your name.

All the answers you can accept
begin there. Rooted, like ideal
children, in that locale where answers
are things you touch, they wear the features
of a world too easy to fail
or be struck dumb. They sing to themselves.
They cheerfully explain that gardens

flourish without you, that the tall,
bright windows that look onto gardens
shine because there is no one in them.
A comfort, an accounting for absence
signed with your own name. You can
walk out into the afternoon's
exact center and disappear,

knowing, now, that what becomes
of you has a place reserved among all
the words and smiles you have arranged
in your best dream. Which is to say

that the world loves you back and is changed
permanently by what you do.
As simple as that. To want some things to live

because they will live anyway,
to look at a photograph
of strangers waving up to you
from a garden somewhere in New Haven,
makes your share of the world possible.
It adds a name to the list. It fills
the sky with the tops of trees and letters.

Prague

Only in the Balkans are there instruments
sad and parti-colored in the right way,
sounding like concertinas still playing
weeks after the Last Judgment and a steady
drizzle gathering on narrow cornices.
Only the Balkan cities are fit to live in.

I am happiest without my life and in cities
of the unmarried who know how to love tyrants
and for how long, until the stern, huge eyes
on the banners fill with tenderness and the steady
drizzle is a shower of good hopes
at a wedding. Think of how I will be dancing then.

Think of the music and the sad, parti-colored
instruments that have survived the world's end
and worse for love of the state, of me, of stern
huge eyes dissolving into tears
in the heaven of banners. I once lost everything
who was the one person I loved in a free city.

In the Balkans I can free her again.
This time, the child will be born. I will teach it
to walk in the damp streets of the history
of cities that ask for nothing except steady
rain, sad instruments, and a tyrant
whose eyes weep tears of joy at our rejoicing.

A Heart's Instruments

I choose the beautiful defeat of one city
sprawled under its dogs and cupolas.
The last century. The orchestras disbanded
into snowy corners. I choose one saint.
She hovers over new snow, fiddling
the ballad and dog's borough of defeat.

Is the government of snow and music
any worse than laws? Are saints any the less dead
in triumph than in defeat? I feel at home
among the beautiful misfortunes and wrong
choices, among the hovering fiddlers,
because I have ruined one place so many times.
I come home, and it is always a burned city.

She sent her body away. You could smell fire.
She buried her words in muslin, her big eyes
in her empty hands. The golden cupolas
turned a sickening black in the woodsmoke.
I felt her boot in her whole heart shattering
my ribs and open jaw. The dogs went crazy.

I am easier than I have ever been.
The snow is the lightest mantle of the law,
and my saint knows me. She fiddles every corner
of the last century into a long dance.

The dogs dance. My wife, killed in the fire,
dances atop the cupolas like white smoke.

I choose this beautiful defeat. I feel
that I am stepping backwards out of a church
into the unmarried, first light on the church steps.
The music is ruined, and everywhere. My heart's
instruments scatter into snowy corners.
Their beautiful misfortune is good history.

The Backyard in August

This drone and heat are the afterlife of one
drawn out, unbalanced sympathy that wrecked
in the tree, in the parched grass, and in the little
fires of insects spitting out of the dark.
The wreckage smolders. It has a low voice.

And what good is a voice and what does it do
in the next life? You make a song out of yours.
I make a prayer and pray it over you,
droning nonsense fit for none to sing.
In no time, the two of us are at home again.

Not strange, the way a yard becomes the hot
field and pressure of the afterworld.
Where else could we have gone but out back,
into the private, fenced air to haunt the wreckage?
What else could we do but sing, pray and keep house?

Eternity is the exhausted revival
of what we feel and cannot keep alive.
I wish it would end. I wish the yard would cool
down into shorter days and routine stillness.
In the soft light, I could clear away

the wreckage, rake it into mounds with the dead
grass and stray leaves blown in from other yards.
By nightfall, I would be in the house, in front
of a whole wall of dark windows. I would pray
the old prayers and watch them drift into your mouth.

III
Clearing Away

For Borges

I will die or think of other words than freedom
and history to bracelet the thin arms of girls
like uncertain wings in air they have not stolen.
I will die or be upheld at this distance
in the just state of trees and civic gardens
of the near future where no one is born equal.

Does everyone remember the same day
on the bus? Do one by one their suddenly
arrowed faces dig into the windows looking
down into the traffic where is no help,
up at a sky that has no bracelets, no freedom?
I am thinking of girls that look like one girl.

I will be dead when I stop thinking and learn
that freedom is one thing apart from history
and that one girl's thin arms are yet another,
civic trees, transport and gardens nothing
but an accidental conspiracy
at one moment where no one is born happy.

Everyone steps down into the street.
There is much to do, and almost all of it
matters to some people. I mean good people,
as worried for the bare sky and the freedom
of thin girls with their impossible, bare arms
like wings as I am. And they go home on a bus.

I will not be living when history
opens the sky and the one girl whose wings
I myself made and placed on her arms
begins to know me. There is no such girl.
She is a better thing to do with freedom
in the real justice where no one is born alive.

Car Radio

An in-joke and the long days faltering
at the edge of fields just visible as we
drive on, the windows shuddering in twilight,
are parts of the songs. And we are travelling
faster all the time, no way to keep
up with them. Between ourselves and the night
coming onto uneasy towns like smoke
the songs are a commitment we do not make
that gets made for us. Our own words reshaped
into the reliable, broken speech of the next
town and all those after it. As we
drive on, we see each one of them escape
us, certain that it will reappear in the context
of another song, the in-joke of the whole country.

Futurist

Thank you for my happy childhood.
A late defector, I am the tallest one
in the newsreels, the only one who waves
as though he were looking into a railyard
or a girl's mirror. And that is what I see—

my hand waving, every window of the cars
filled with Anne and the cautionary, hopeless greeting
of her eyes looking into the East.
I have gone there and betrayed everything
for the chance to sing ballads to empty streets.

I am so glad my childhood was happy.
It was a nut-brown quiet under high lamps,
and then spring, and then almost a marriage.
Anne emptied every window of the cars
all at once, and then I was no child.

Then it was time to come here, out of the lamplight.
The cameras rolled and I waved, the tallest
of the late defectors with no language and songs
named for tyrants. History teaches us:
Mayakovsky died; there are always cowards and girls.

The Next Marriage

Will it reach down, an open mouth of sparrows
and mock orange? Will it leave a taste of oil
heavy through each day for months afterwards?

I've taken a room. It looks out over half
of a big lake and no faces ever come
to the window—only the lake view, detached

from the half sky and the shadow of birds' throats.
Quiet enough in the meantime. All night,
the window is a ghost of the furniture

standing on lake water, the wet moon
a ghost's uncertain heart. I think that death
is a half lake and that the view from there

opens under sky like a sparrow's mouth
on pure sound and air tasting of orange oil.
A half dozen marriages and none could walk

over dark water and not one's heart rises
in any one room's darkening window now.
Is it so wrong to want as many lives

as even a room has? In the best one, Anne
did not die, high-shouldered in the forties' style,
in a hat that made her brow a little candle.

All morning, the lake is easy in its better
half. Birds open their small mouths to the half sky,
and I am a day closer to the next marriage.

It's all a matter of days—what people wear,
what they sound like, what flowers bloom from their mouths.
I like to see Anne under her little hat.

Charleston

1.

It begins in a freak storm and then
goes on for months, into summer. Taking
the same roads I take, stopping at all
the same attractions (the live bears, the white
battlefield memorials), it gets

south, bright with that odd lustre of clippings
stuck in letters from home. "June Gala!
Everyone will gather and then move on
to a reception." Someplace south. There,
wind shakes in the palmettos and I stop.

A part of anyone can be wrapped
up in a particular fear or some
design lifted out of the weather
of one place or one spring day. That part
revises things in advance. It makes

them sad or ridiculous before they
happen. The weddings, the reunions
fall flat. Even in Charleston where, tonight,
they are preparing a bungalow
for me and the summer is already

moving inland over the sea wall,
something fails and stays in the air, waiting.

It is like a cloud I have sent on
ahead of me in my sleep, for comfort.
And so there are two clouds mixed up in

the near future: one to travel with me,
another to wait, hovering near
my place by the sea wall. Beginning in
storms which are themselves a gathering
of clippings and promises, they take up

months, whole years sometimes, between the two
of them. What remains is an interval.
I step out of my bungalow by
the sea, and then it starts. The reception
comes to life under a clear blue sky.

2.

All the special events I can recall
seem to have happened in one place whose prospects
embarrass me by their plainness. Even so,
I liked it there and want to go back more
than anything. For fun, I think of it
as Charleston. There, the occasions that deserved
glamour can have it and can be relived
under the bright marquees that ought to have shone
for them the first time. Loving an event
or place gets tricky as time goes by. You can't
help wanting to change it, to endow it with those
qualities which, only now, you see
it needed. Memory preserves things by adding
to them. Each year, the couples at my wedding

dance more gracefully and wear better clothes.
The streets of my birthplace widen into grand
boulevards whose lights move like flying candles
across the night sky. The trick is to go back
each time as ready to be amazed as moved
by what you'd love to remember and then be
amazed. That way, everything can keep a step
ahead of the explanations, the regrets
that are the worst part of memory and the biggest
as things stand now. My choice of a new locale
proves that. At my wedding, as at all the events
I've tried to bring to Charleston, no marquees
shone, no streets grew wide to make room for dancing.
That is the center of what happened. Now,
even that can be revised. There is
a way of remembering that lays on years
of bright, fluent surfaces that move and cloud
whatever they're fixed to. As a kind of enchantment
over time, it moves the past along. It leads
a dance to the brink of where I should be next,
attired for anything under a clear blue sky.

3.

Moving among them, I can only
recognize the other guests as gracious
versions of themselves, as amazing
as they are suddenly familiar, now
that I remember wanting them here

with me by the sea wall so often, and
now that all the occasions they've danced

at shine in them and in the way they move.
In Charleston, the past recaptures what
it needs, then shines. I've known it would, always.

I've known that, eventually, there
would come that interval between the one
kind of cloudiness and the other
(the past that waits, the past that always moves
just as I do), and that, arriving,

it would be my chance to get everything
south where it all ought to have happened
all the time. Only movement compensates
for failure. The special events that,
for whatever reasons, did not come off,

can be gathered into a gracious
blur now and moved beneath the wind that shakes
in the palmettos. Too changed to be
sad quite yet, the weddings, the reunions
anticipate my changing ideas

of them, seeming to shift in that dreamlike
attitude of people standing still
on a moving sidewalk. The flawless guests
trace a constellation of revised
moments, recaptured as they are needed,

between my bungalow and the sea
wall. The pattern comes shining through the blur.
It lasts just long enough for me to learn
how to remember it later and how
to be amazed by its perfection.

Beloved Author and the New State

The parked barrows of the infirm at Lourdes
are no book. There is nothing to read there.
No faith, nor even the most pitiful
sick man hauled to the shrine on little fists
varies the routine, meagre dole. The only
excuse for pain invents happy pilgrims, cures
pity. It is everything with no voice
and dances on little fists as I read on.

That is how you come in, still finishing
the laugh you began under new curls, ready
to dance us both out of line into the sad
glamour of an illness with no saint.
Without charity, the wealth of false hope never
fails. I am alone with you, and dying.
I am terribly interesting, and you
will write my name in an expensive book.

If you could only stop laughing. If the dance
could actually begin, charity
would never match us step for step and I
might never see Lourdes. But your book and picture,
under your new curls, have no future.
Illness surrounds memory with its own text
no one finishes. There is no excuse.
I am on my fists in line, nothing to read there.

Thirties

Dans la grande maison de vitres . . .

—RIMBAUD

Everything is becoming beautifully slim,
the warm night sounds thinning to no one's voice
like a small radio in the smallest room
of a hotel on the Boston Common with no view.

It is interregnum always now.
The doors onto the Common stagger at street level,
never finding the public staircase
down to the river and the girl there

I met for the first time as she took my picture.
I smiled, then, for what I must now call joy,
the source of the Nile, of the Charles. Interregnum
always is every door staggering

into the aimless circles of night couples
and of their small radios inside the Common.
They have perfectly good rooms to go to.
They have an answer to every night sound but nothing

to stop themselves becoming so thin,
so hopelessly reed-like, none will need a room
but only a narrow ledge in the dark with no view,
not even a radio there or a framed snapshot.

I used to find staircases everywhere.
New England was full of rich men

who found them in Europe, bought them and rebuilt them
on estates that became public parks.

I would take a bus, walk down the stairs
and a girl would photograph me. Behind me,
a lithic crescent of river loosed
atoms of real glass into the air.

That was the future. That was a girl
I married and outlived after her voice
expired ten flights up in a hotel.
I have a perfectly good room to go to.

I prefer the interregnum of night couples
in darkening circles along narrow paths
and their small radios. So beautifully slim,
their futures catwalk atoms of real glass.

Emily Dickinson's Mirror, Amherst

Its flecked surface a map of disappearing islands,
the glass imposes a narrowing, flat sense
of time and limited space upon the room
at all angles. Looking into it head on,
I feel contained and ready to understand
the short lines' skewed New England syntax mouthed
into so strict a frame. A discipline
of words arrayed for the bridal and no groom
wanted. In each of us, there must be one
oracular, strait emptiness a hand's
breadth across that is ourselves in proud
fear, looking into our own eyes for doctrine
and the one audience whose accents we can
share wholly. The purist's God. Pride's mirror and island.

Maestro

The final curiosity of one
near death was all the future. He
remarked upon a window, how the sun
defined it, how a certain oddity
of light could change the view: from an urban brick
into a seascape, or from sky into
a woman's face, like Anne's among the rocks
in Mantua. He talked about the blue

effect of oxygen on dinner. When
the lights went out, he counted rings to make
an average, every night a different
report, and every morning numbers. Awake
at dawn, he listened to the nurses kid
each other over handsome patients. Death
was probably a fraction. What you did
was think; you drew a pair of lungs; you breathed.

Descriptive Quality

Spite the wind. Call it the air that falls
out of trees, the colorless, blank underside
of what you see on the drive home on highways.
Spite is the isolation that scars. It scores
the cutting and bending air with sharp sounds.

In all the noise, accommodations come hard.
I get out of the car. I remember
to need to live in a house and to describe
things fairly, in the dull words and inconstant,
clumsy stories it is easy to change.

What accounts for this? I think the wind does.

Spite the wind. Describe it wrong, knowing
each partisan inaccuracy to be
a blow against the treaty of air that bends
solid, helpless things into stick figures
and then mistakes the little sticks for words.

I like to live in a house. I want to step
inside and tell children what I saw from the car—
all fiction. I saw nothing like the wind
and no air stirred so quickly the highway changed
into the luminous underside of leaves frozen white.

What accounts for this? I think my name does.

Malice is the country home of names
and of the isolations they describe.
All the sad mishaps unfold out there
in every room of the huge house, in weak light.
The shadows lunge into silence. Everyone

except a vacant-eyed young man drifts off
into the twilit, deep garden. He lifts
a china bowl with both hands and calls it *flower,*
shattered, twilit leaf, or any other
solid, helpless thing that he has seen.

Raft of the Medusa

Some things are even more important
and we point frantically in that direction
toward the vertical music of landfall.
Think of us, then, as the huge victims of shipwreck
revived in the tall studio of a painter
in north light. We are never bigger than that.
And we are overshadowed even then
by some things taller, far inland with our houses.

No sense putting the blame on Géricault.
A man's sheer size is no bigger than his death
no matter if he is painted as a giant
among other giants on a cannibal raft.
You need to look away from the north light.
You need to find drowned men small and living
inland in the shady use of affection
for things deathless for no reason.

That is where you find things more important
than shipwreck. Among the rafts of light novels.
In corners of windowseats that look down
onto the front walk between dark leaves
folded like messages. A long time
before anyone is shipwrecked, he has chosen
part of a novel or some green window
never to die, never to let him die.

He is eaten on the raft of the Medusa.
Or he drowns in aftertimes in a tilted bed

beneath the cannibal comforts of dry land.
The north light shows up nothing of this. The tall
studio of the painter is too busy
with corpses pointing frantically in one direction
towards a vertical music he does not paint—
a folded message deathless for no reason.

The Contemporary Poetry Series

Edited by Paul Zimmer

The Contemporary Poetry Series

Edited by Bin Ramke